WELCOME TO CHINA WITH SESAME STREET

CHRISTY PETERSON

Lerner Publications ◆ Minneapolis

In this series, *Sesame Street* characters help readers learn about other countries' people, cultures, landscapes, and more. These books connect friends around the world while giving readers new tools to become smarter, kinder friends. Pack your bags and take a fun-filled look at your world with your funny, furry friends from *Sesame Street*.

—Sincerely, the Editors at Sesame Street

TABLE OF CONTENTS

WELCOME TO CHINA!

Ni hao!
That means "hello" in Mandarin! My name is Lily. I live in China. This is the Great Wall of China!

4

China is a country in Asia. There are many wonderful things that make China special. The people who live there are a lot like you!

WHERE IN THE WORLD IS CHINA?

China and Surrounding Area

RUSSIA

AFGHANISTAN
KAZAKHSTAN
TAJIKISTAN
KYRGYZSTAN
MONGOLIA
PAKISTAN
NORTH KOREA
Beijing ★
YELLOW SEA
CHINA
INDIA
NEPAL
EAST CHINA SEA
BHUTAN
TAIWAN
Miles
0 200 400
0 200 400 600
Kilometers
PACIFIC OCEAN
MYANMAR
VIETNAM
LAOS
SOUTH CHINA SEA

NORTH AMERICA

ATLANTIC OCEAN

PACIFIC OCEAN

SOUTH AMERICA

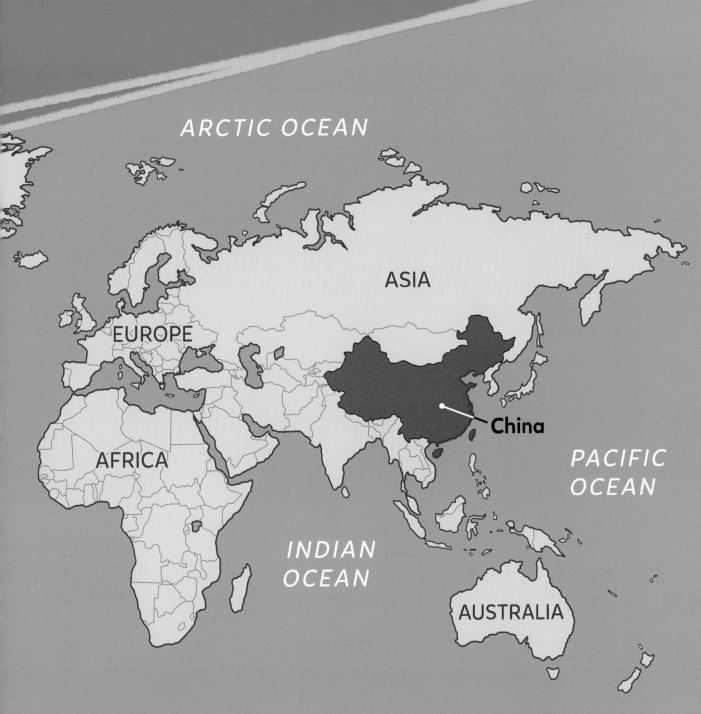

ARCTIC OCEAN

ASIA

EUROPE

China

AFRICA

PACIFIC
OCEAN

INDIAN
OCEAN

AUSTRALIA

SOUTHERN OCEAN

China is a very big country. There are deserts, forests, farmland, and mountains. The Himalayan Mountains are often called the roof of the world.

China has more people than any other country.

There are many types of homes in China. Some families live in modern, tall apartment buildings. Others live in homes that look like they are from long ago.

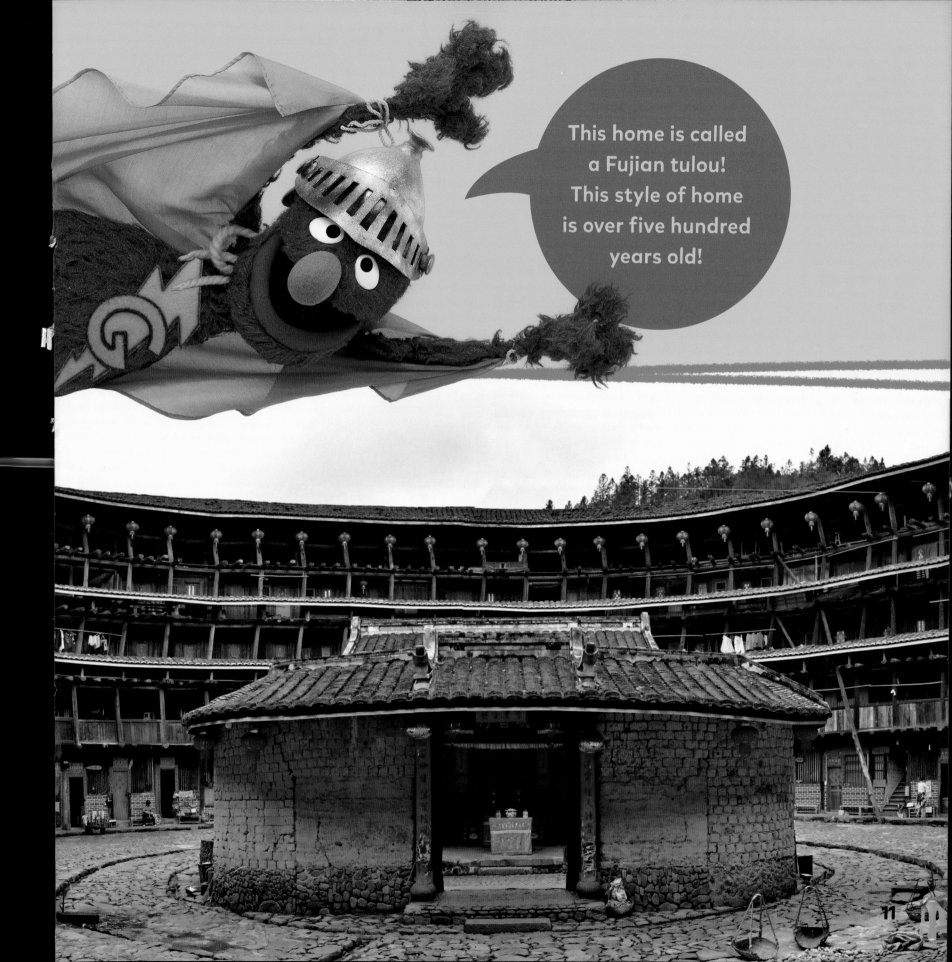

In China, rice and tofu are popular.
Sweet dumplings are a favorite for
many Chinese people.

Many Chinese people eat with chopsticks. I want to learn how to use chopsticks too.

13

Lunar New Year is an important holiday. People travel to be with their families. They hang red decorations.

In China, students wear uniforms to school.
Each school's uniform is different.

After school, students can play sports or take classes in painting, music, chess, and more.

I have ballet practice after school!

Children in China spend a lot of time with their grandparents. They read and play together.

Families in China like to play games together, just like families around the world.

I'm learning to play Chinese chess.

Flag of China

FAST FACTS

Continent: Asia

Capital city: Beijing

Population: 1.4 billion

Languages: Mandarin, Wu, and Yue

GLOSSARY

Chinese chess: a game where players try to capture the "king" piece of the other player

dumpling: a small mass of dough with filling or stuffing cooked by boiling or steaming

Fujian tulou: a walled village that houses more than one family

modern: common in the present day

uniform: an outfit worn by members of a particular group

LEARN MORE

DK staff. *China through Time: A 2,500-Year Journey along the World's Greatest Canal*. London: DK Children, 2020.

Press, J. P. *Welcome to Mandarin Chinese with Sesame Street*. Minneapolis: Lerner Publications, 2020.

Sebra, Richard. *It's Chinese New Year!* Minneapolis: Lerner Publications, 2017.

INDEX

Photo Acknowledgments

Image credits: Sofiaworld/Shutterstock.com, pp. 4–5; Laura K. Westlund/Independent Picture Service, pp. 6–7, 21; thianchai sitthikongsak/Moment/Getty Images, p. 8; amenic181/Shutterstock.com, p. 9; leungchopan/Shutterstock.com, p. 10; Lao Ma/Shutterstock.com, p. 11; KUNG MIN JU/Shutterstock.com, p. 12; Heng Lim/Shutterstock.com, p. 13; Krunja/Shutterstock.com, p. 14; chee gin tan/E+/Getty Images, p. 15; Ding Genhou/Xinhua/Alamy Stock Photo, p. 16; imtmphoto/Shutterstock.com, p. 18; XiXinXing/Shutterstock.com, p. 19; BJI/Blue Jean Images/Getty Images, p. 20.

Cover: Sergii Rudiuk/Shutterstock.com (top); aphotostory/Shutterstock.com (bottom).

Lerner Publications Company
An imprint of Lerner Publishing Group, Inc.
241 First Avenue North
Minneapolis, MN 55401 USA

For reading levels and more information, look up this title at www.lernerbooks.com.

Main body text set in Mikado a Regular.
Typeface provided by HVD Fonts.

Editor: Andrea Nelson
Lerner team: Sue Marquis

Library of Congress Cataloging-in-Publication Data

Names: Peterson, Christy, author.
Title: Welcome to China with Sesame Street / Christy Peterson.
Description: Minneapolis, MN: Lerner Publications, [2022] | Series: Sesame Street friends around the world | Includes bibliographical references and index. | Audience: Ages 4–8 | Audience: Grades K–1 | Summary: "China is home to almost 1.5 billion people—the biggest population of any country in the world. Readers can learn about Lunar New Year, ancient architecture, and more about the culture of China with Sesame Street friends"—Provided by publisher.
Identifiers: LCCN 2020046247 (print) | LCCN 2020046248 (ebook) | ISBN 9781728424378 (library binding) | ISBN 9781728431529 (paperback) | ISBN 9781728430478 (ebook)
Subjects: LCSH: China—Juvenile literature. | China—Social life and customs—Juvenile literature.
Classification: LCC DS706 .P46 2021 (print) | LCC DS706 (ebook) | DDC 951—dc23

LC record available at https://lccn.loc.gov/2020046247
LC ebook record available at https://lccn.loc.gov/2020046248

Manufactured in the United States of America
1-49307-49423-3/11/2021